Welcome to the first Colouring Book created from the Cyndilu's Photography.
This book is dedicated to my children who love to color as much as I do
- ok at least some of them do!
Enjoy this first book - there are more to come!
Yay... What a fun way to share some photography
and
the landscapes of New Zealand.

All Pages are created directly from the Original Photography of Cyndilu Miller
Copyright © 2019 by Cyndilu Miller and beBOLDyou™ Publishing

Cover Design: Cyndilu Miller

All Rights Reserved.

No part of this publication may be reproduced, distributed, or transmitted in any form or by any means, including photocopying, recording, electronic or mechanical methods, or by any information storage and retrieval system, without the prior written permission of the publisher and author, except the case of brief quotations embodied in critical reviews and certain other non-commercial uses permitted by copyright law.

ISBN: 9781653007325 - Colouring Book
Independently published:
beBOLDyou™ Publishing
10 Bell Street
Owaka 9535
New Zealand

Website:
www.beboldyou.com
Email:
beboldyou@gmail.com
Cyndilu's Photography FB Page
https://www.facebook.com/cyndilusphotos/

The southernmost point of the South Island of New Zealand is often thought to be Invercargill or Bluff but in actuality Slope Point. This is one of the easiest locations to visit as it is a nice gentle walk across private farmland.

When you think of New Zealand you often think of sheep and this colouring book is full of them as we walked down to the signpost we were blessed with passing by the beautiful sheep in the paddock which visitors are granted permission to walk through. It's about a 20 minute walk across the farmland brings you to the yellow signpost which lets you know you are now closer to the South Pole than to the Equator! So fun.

Not only do you get to see the sheep, but you also arrive at a lovely rugged coast line. The mixture of the cliffs and the rolling farmland next to the deep and wide ocean make for some stunning views.

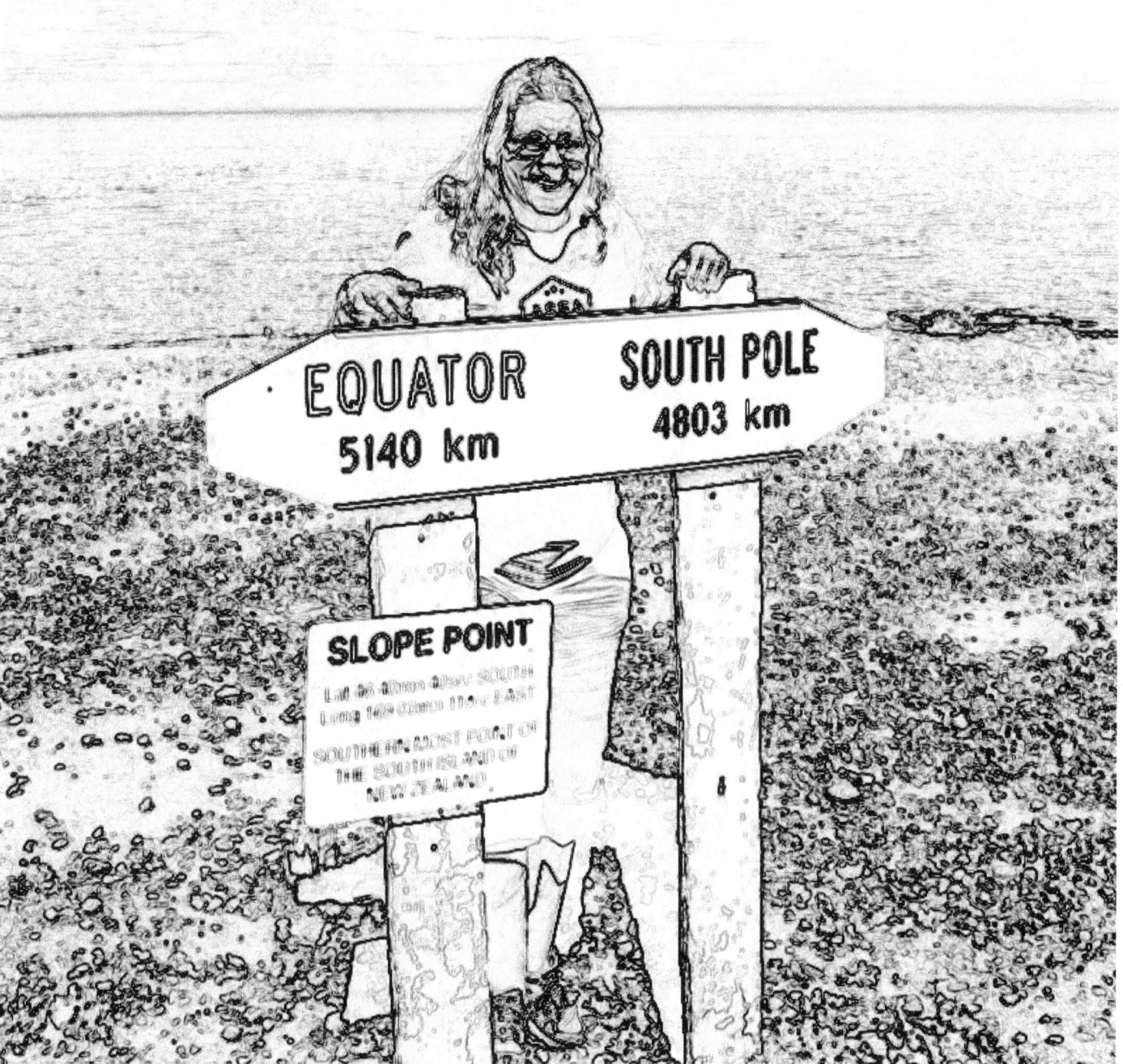

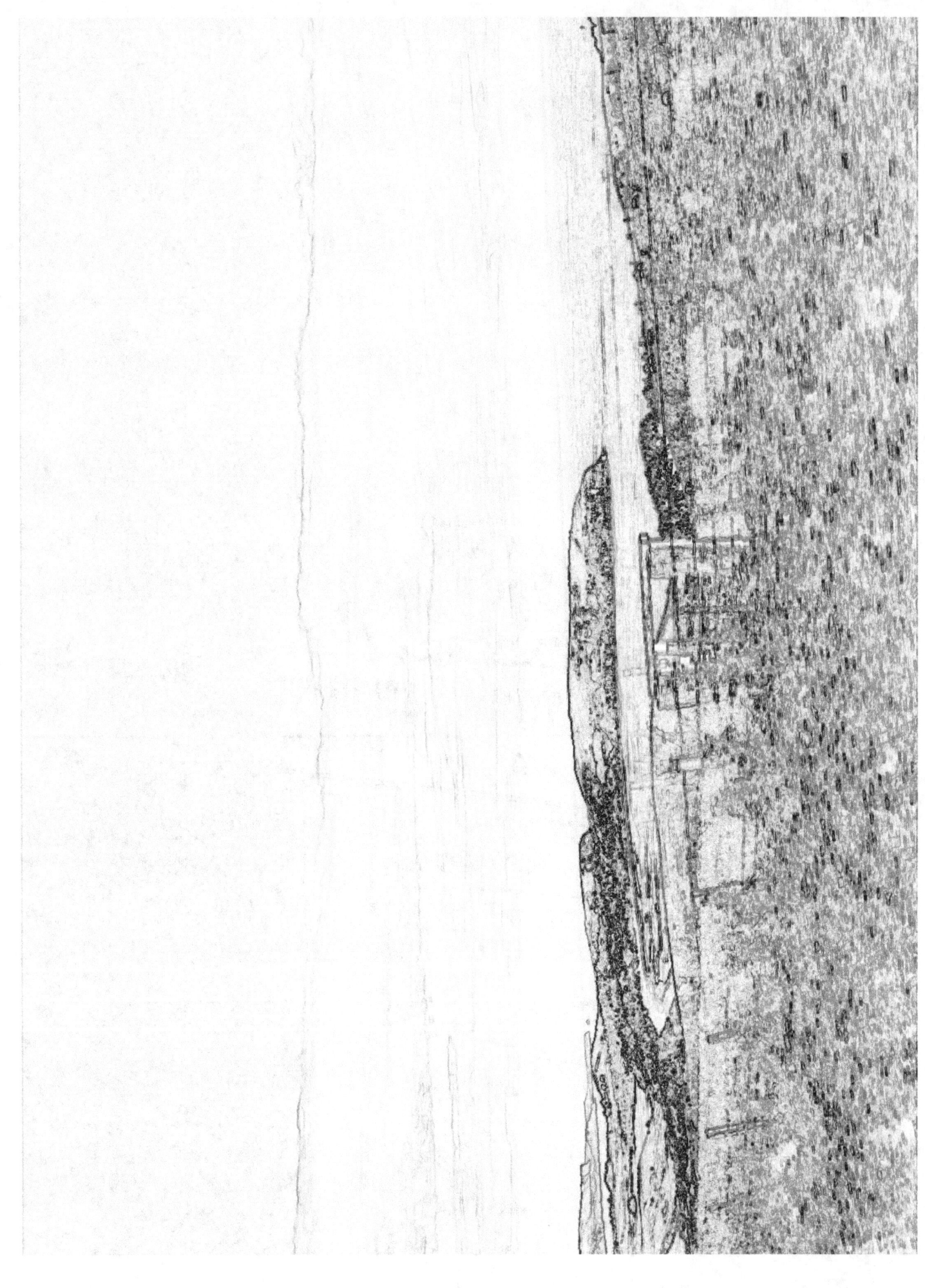

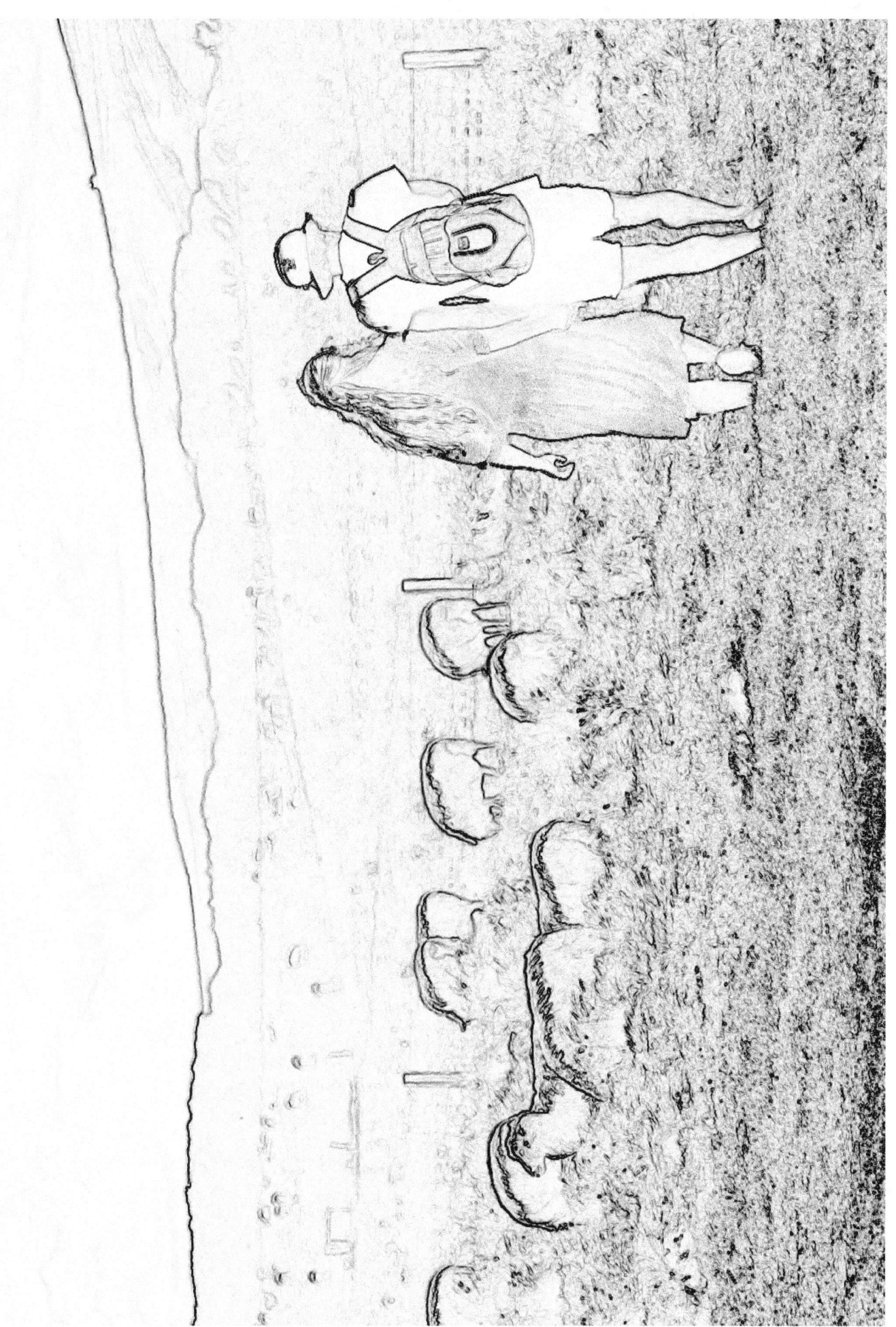

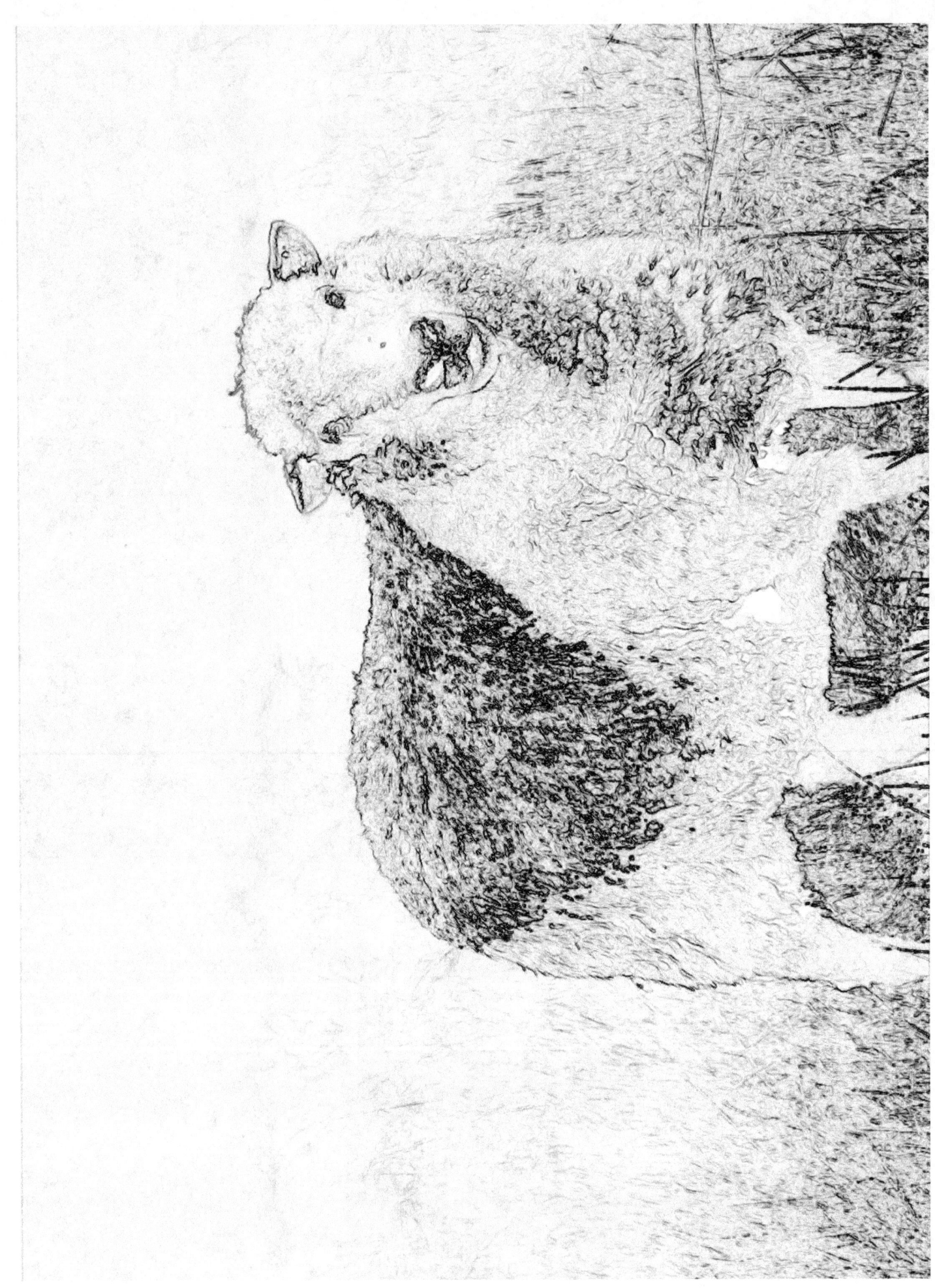

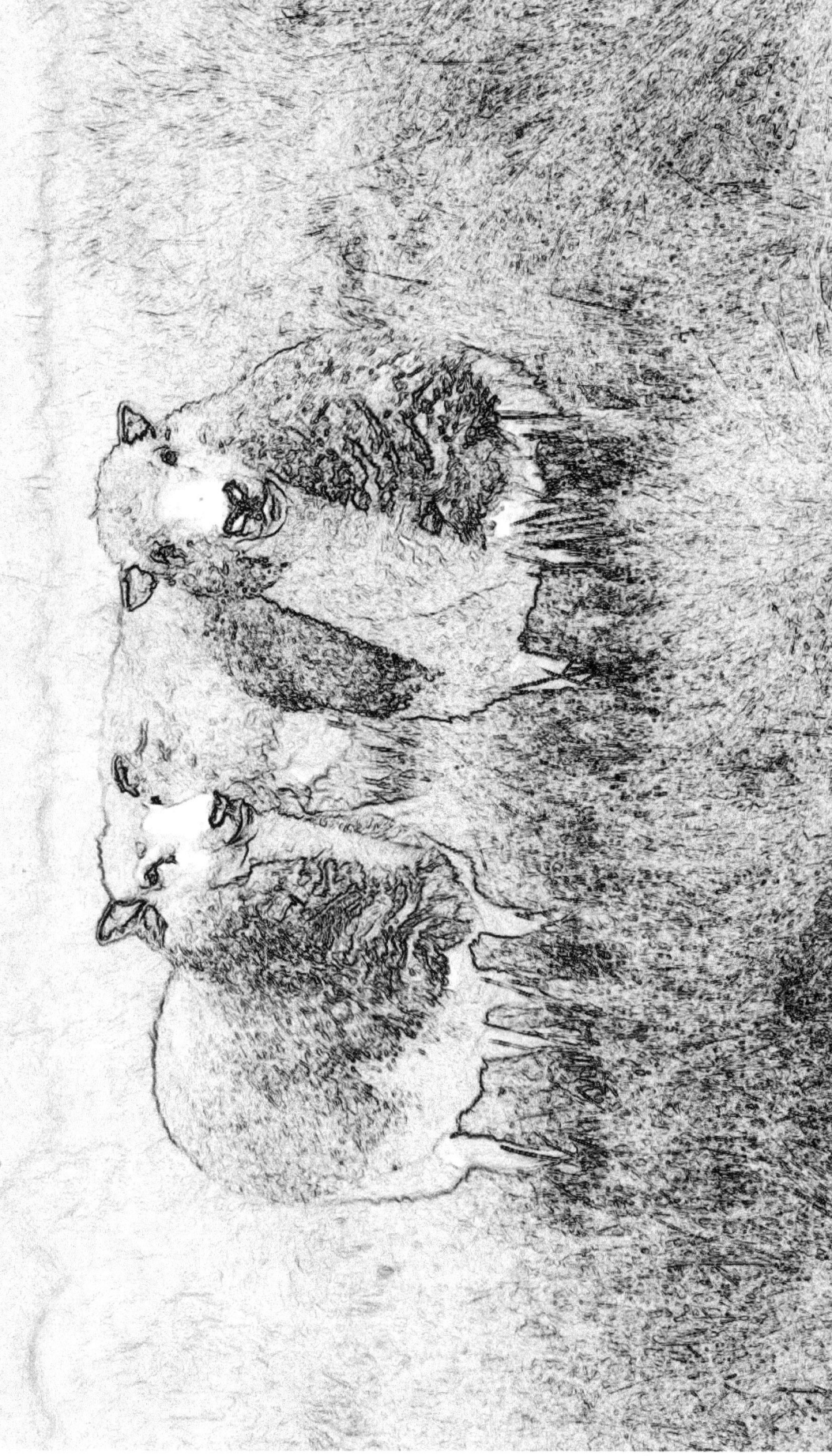

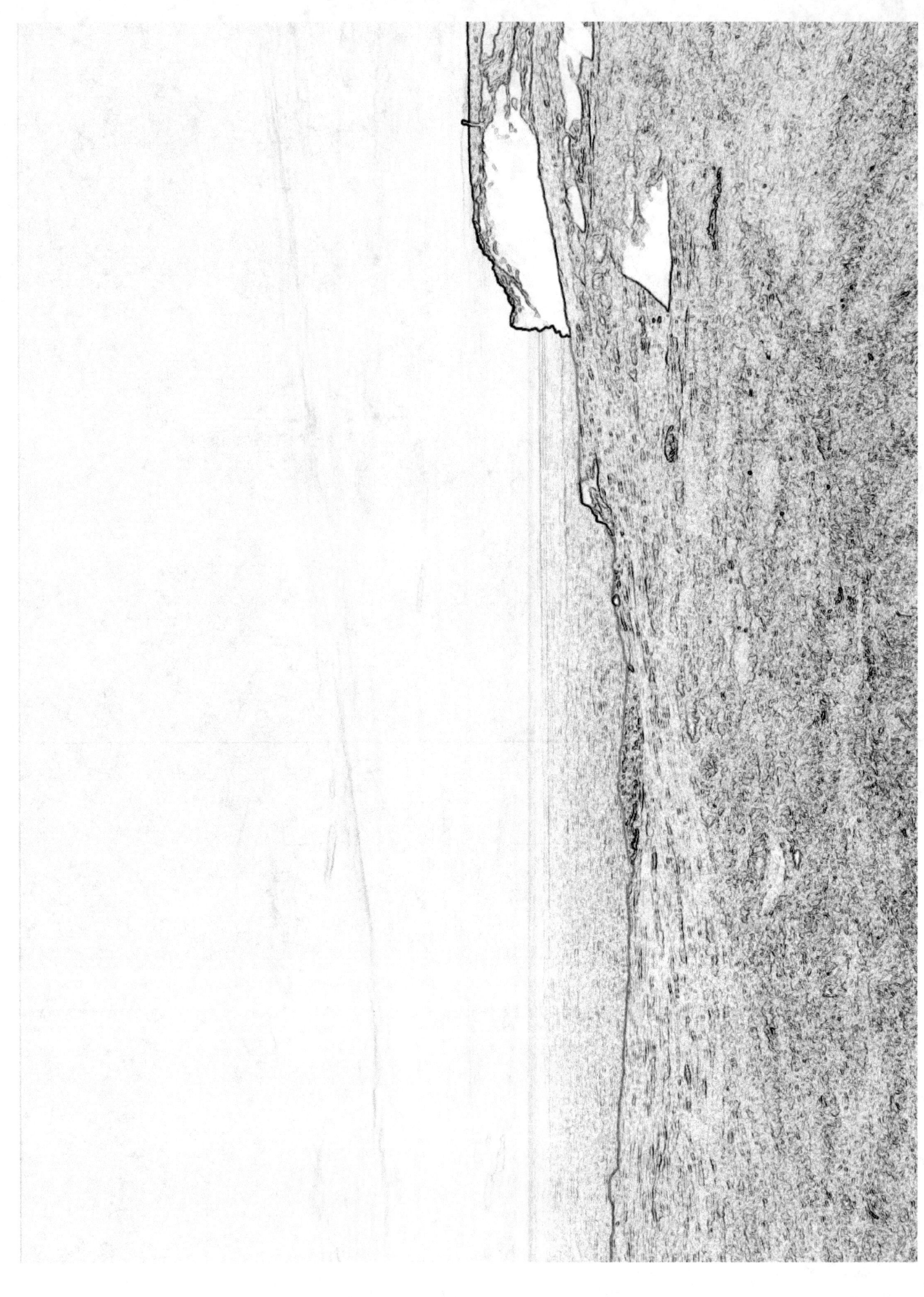

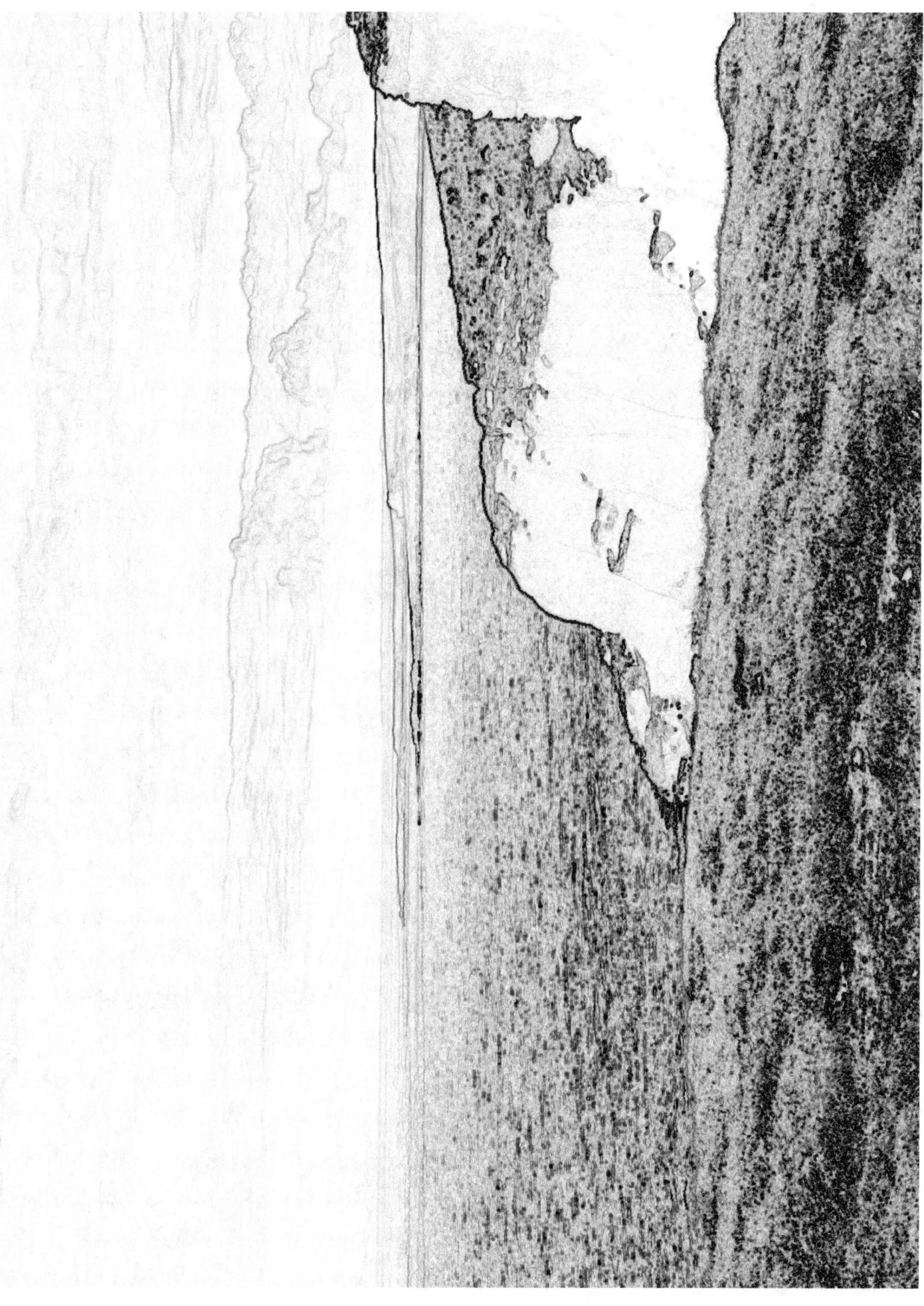

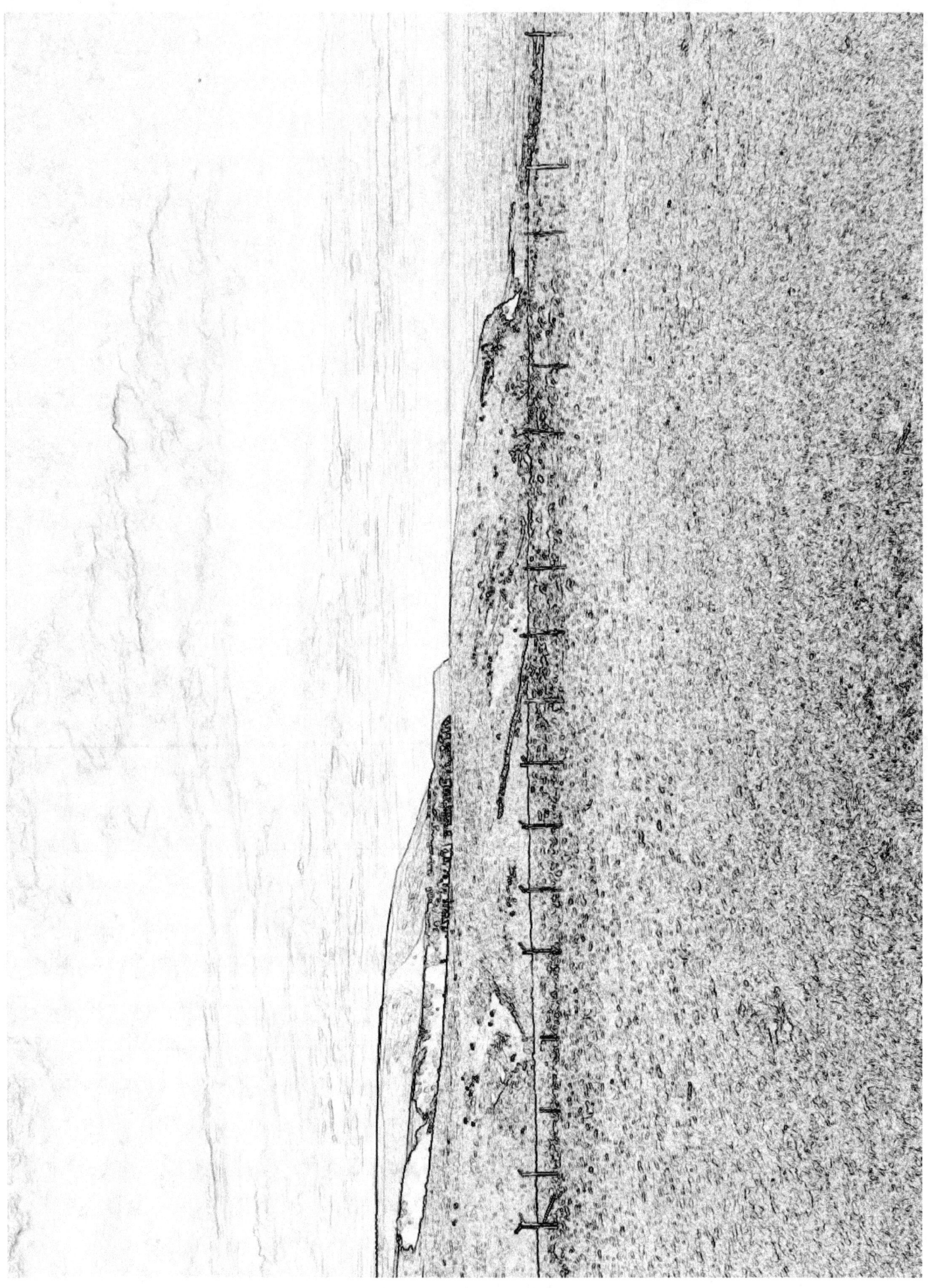

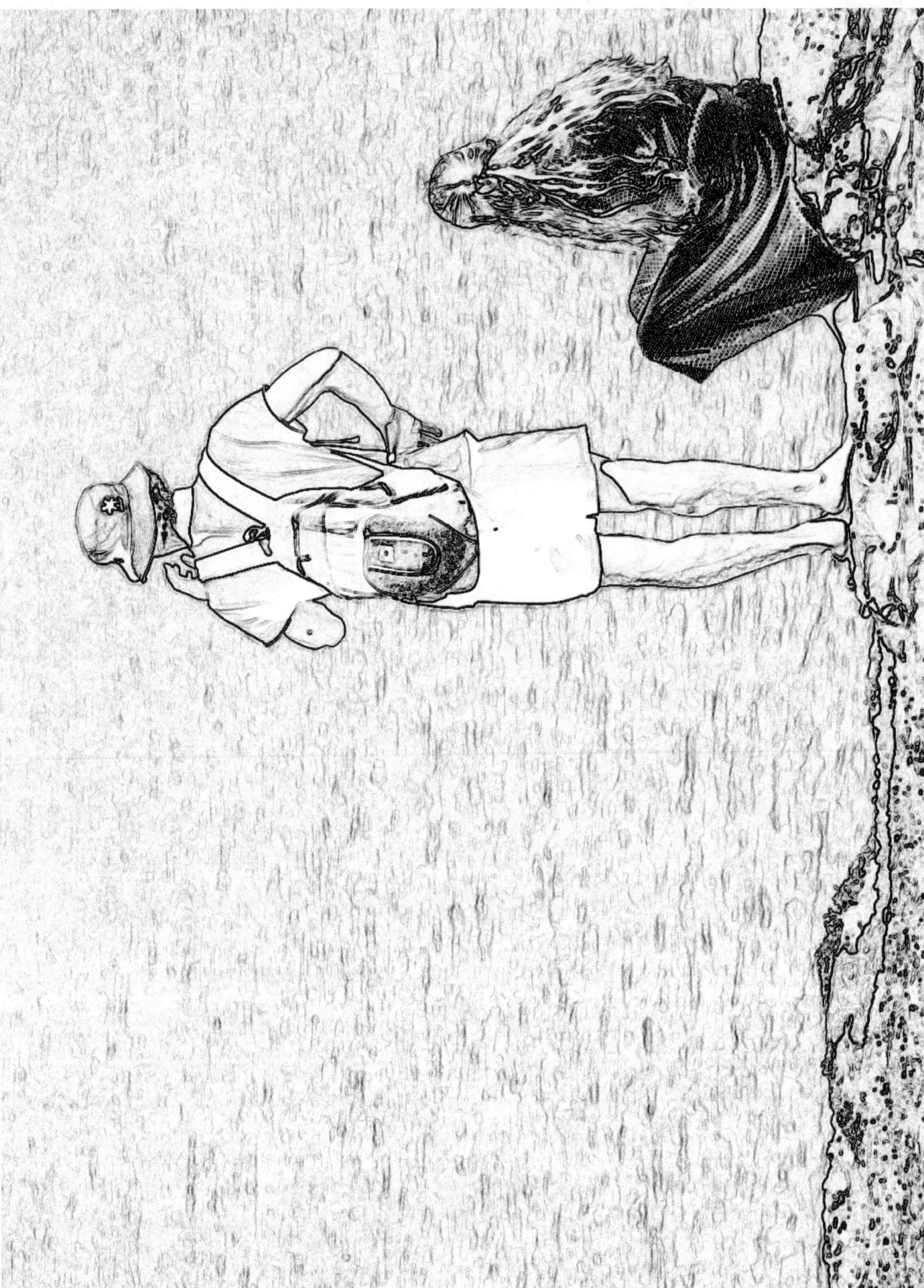

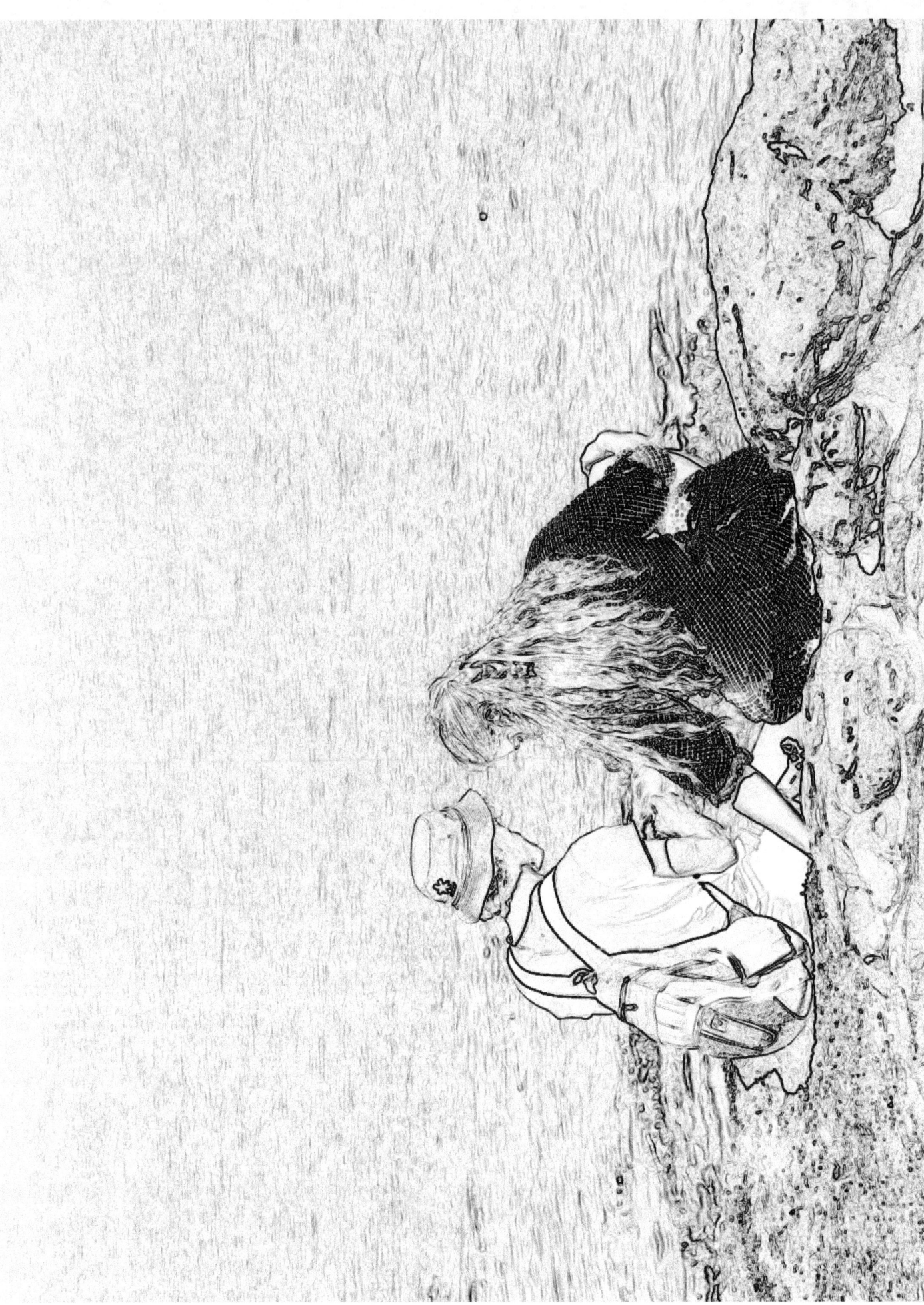

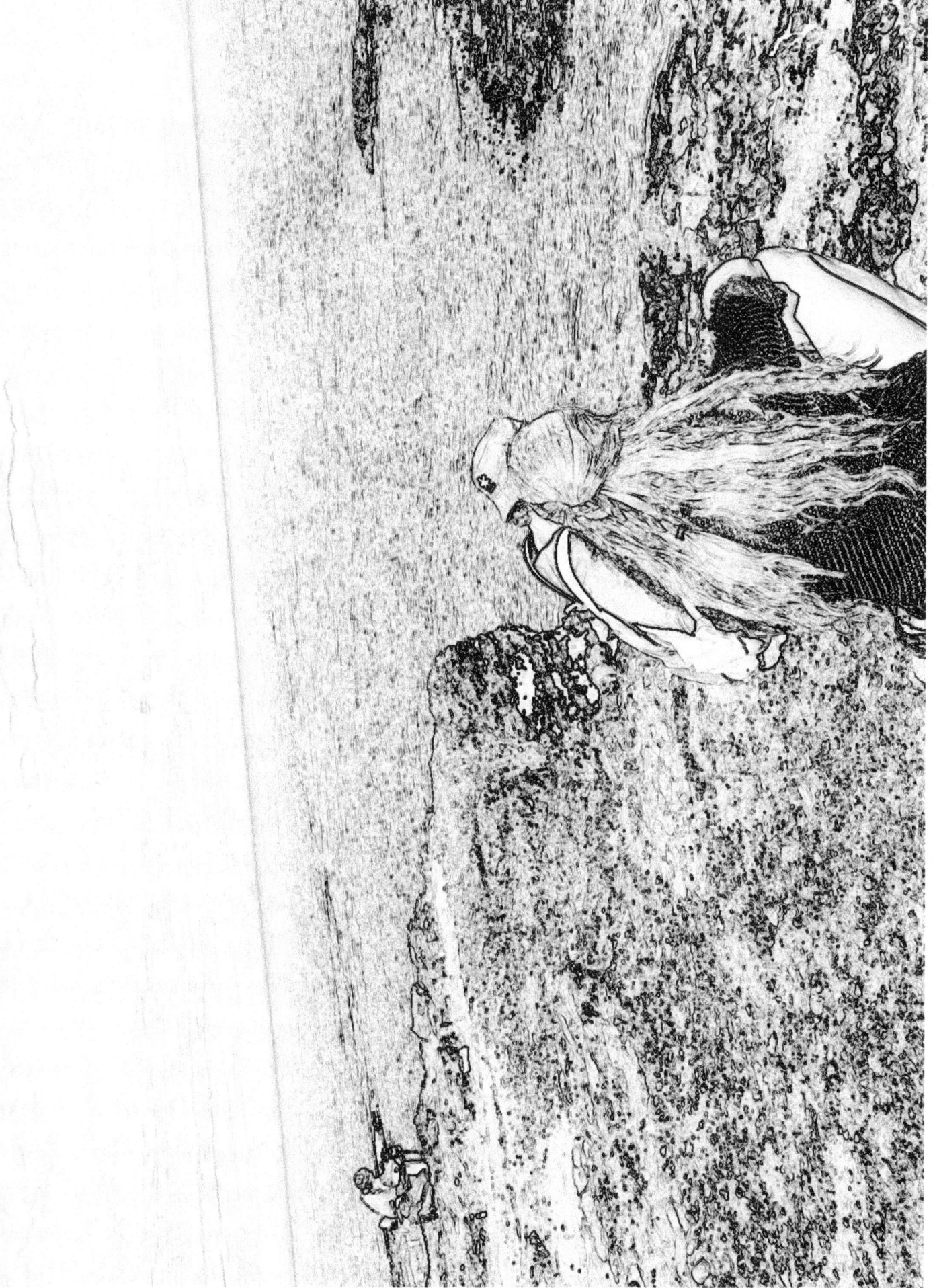

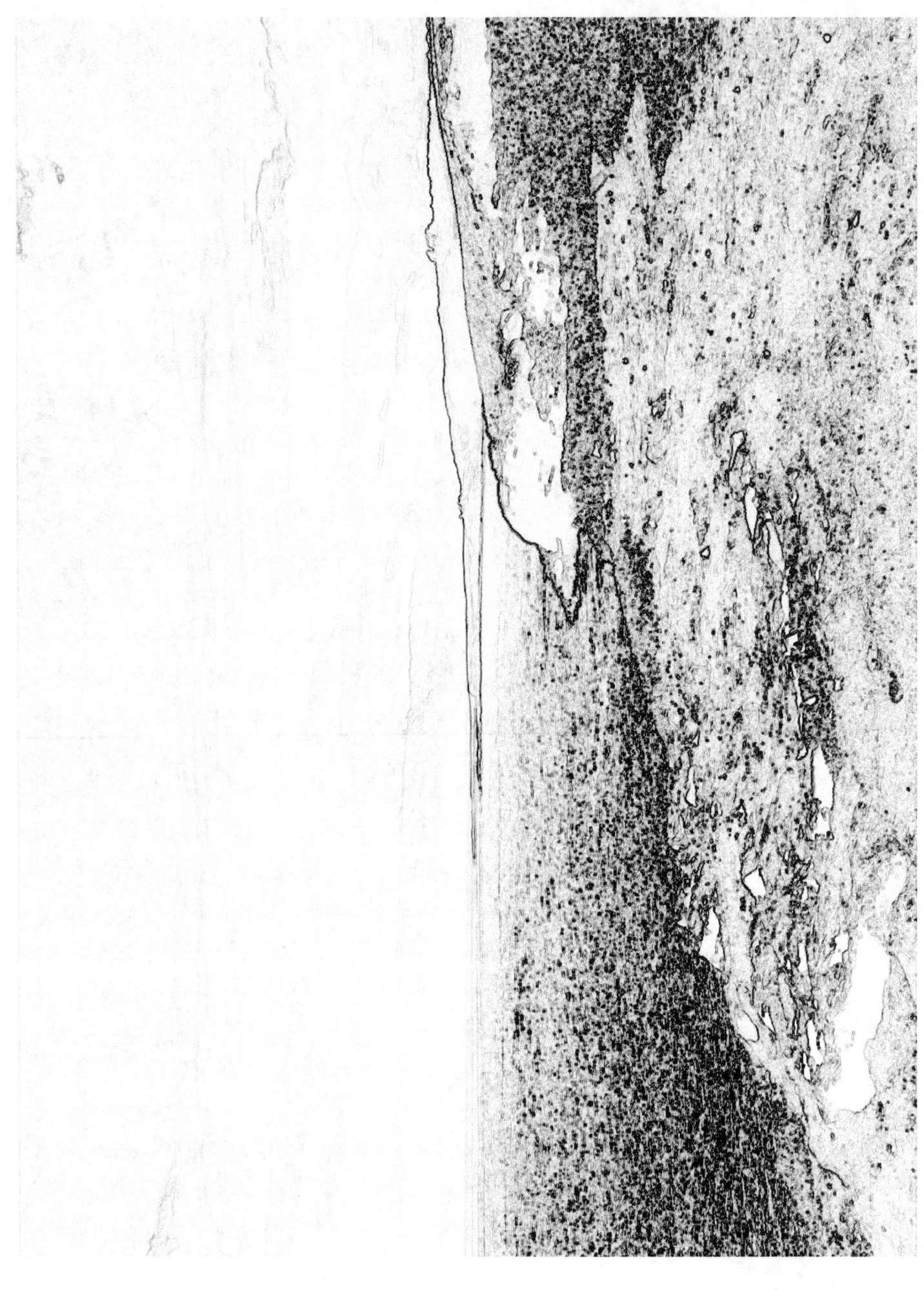

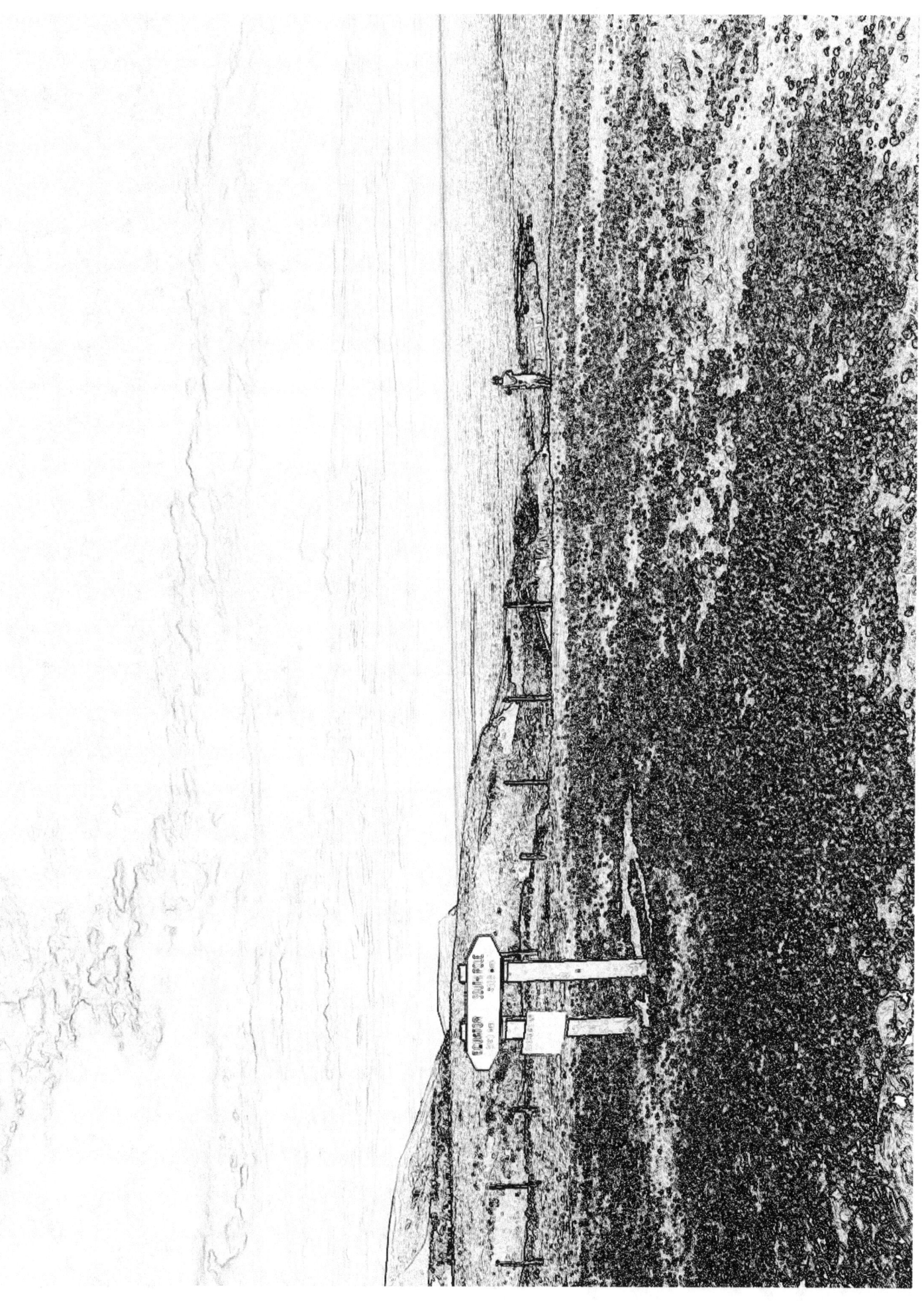

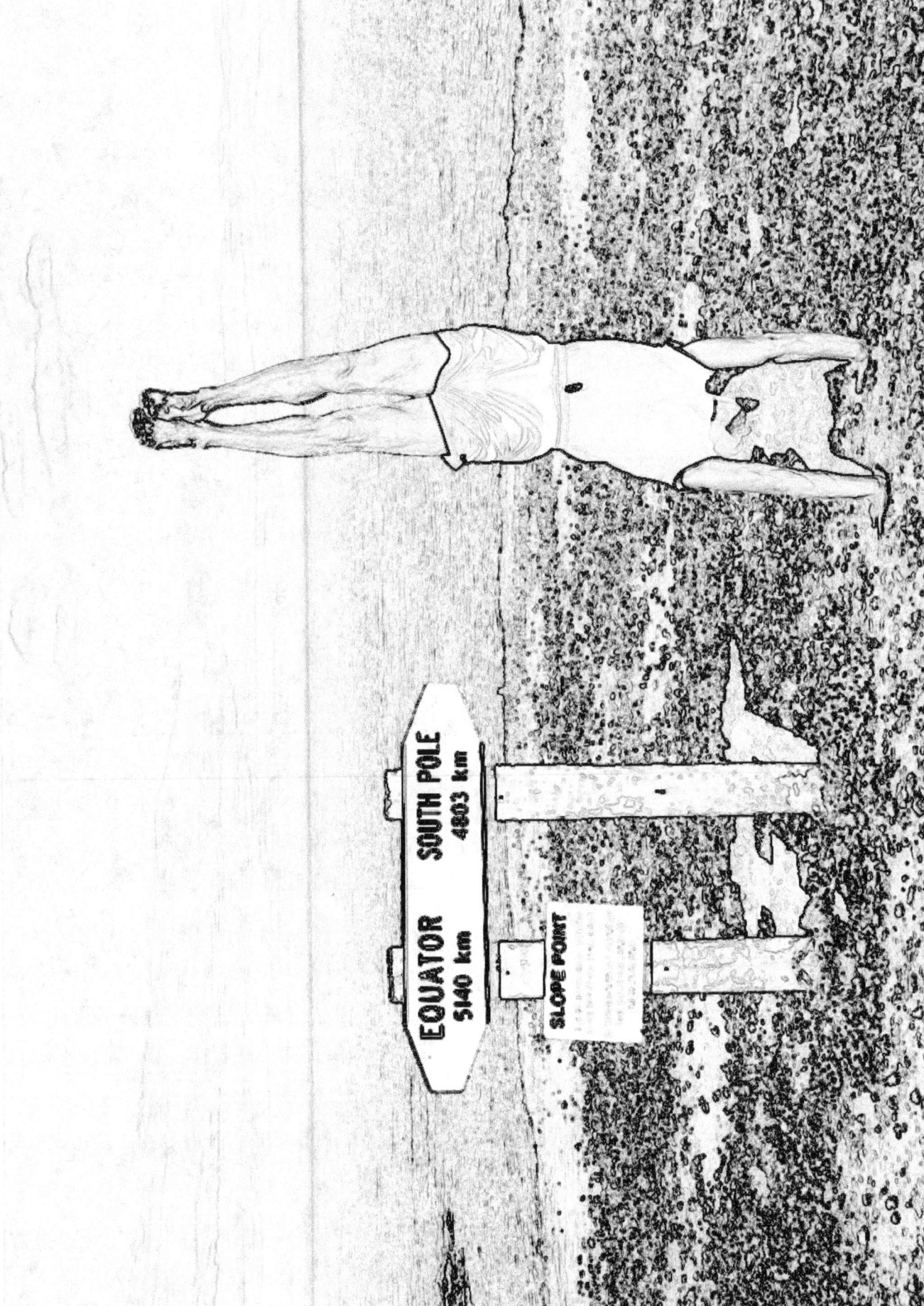

SOUTH POLE 4803 km

EQUATOR 5140 km

SLOPE POINT

Lat 46 40min 40sec SOUTH
Long 169 00min 11sec EAST

SOUTHERN MOST POINT OF
THE SOUTH ISLAND OF
NEW ZEALAND.

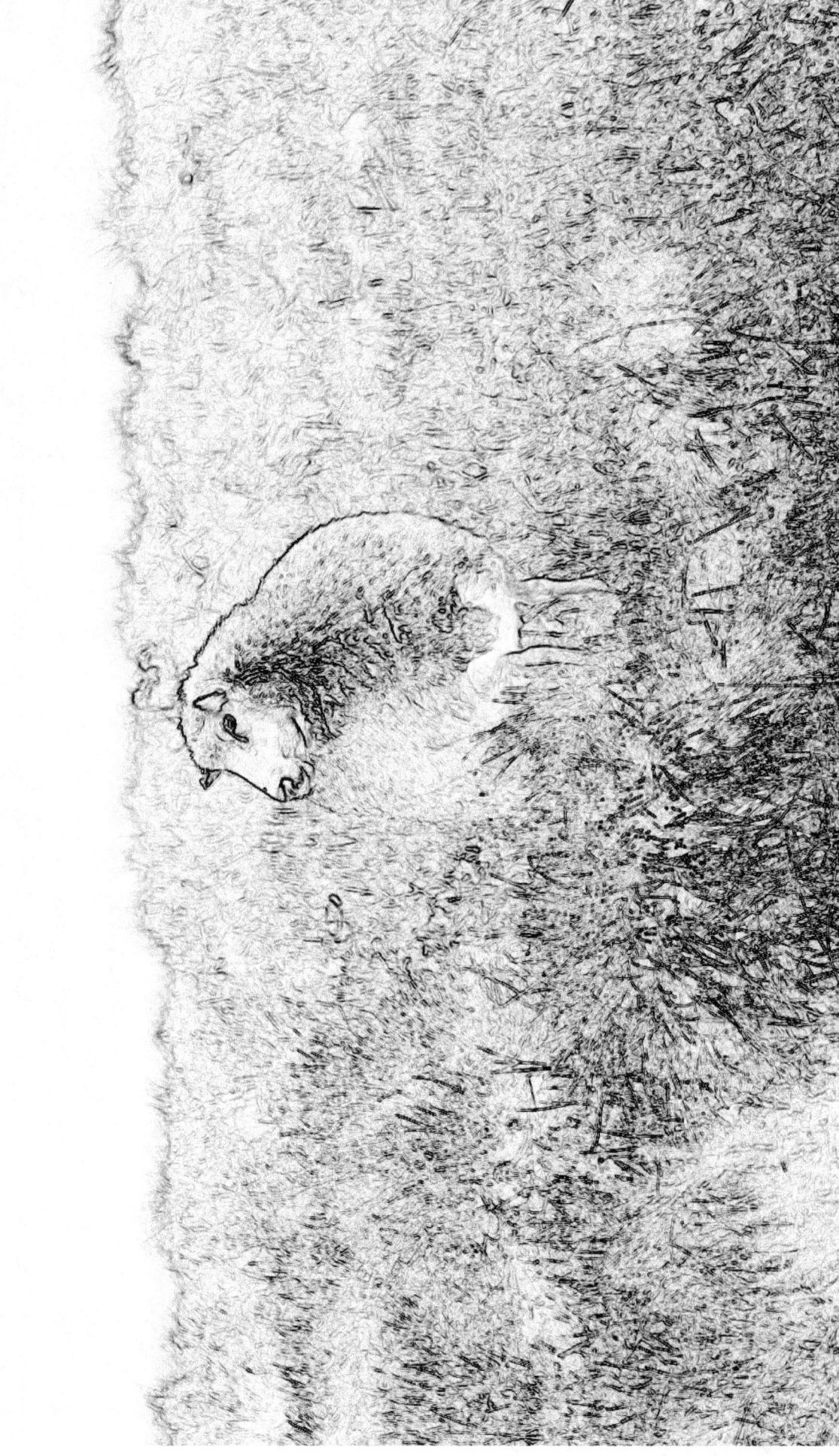

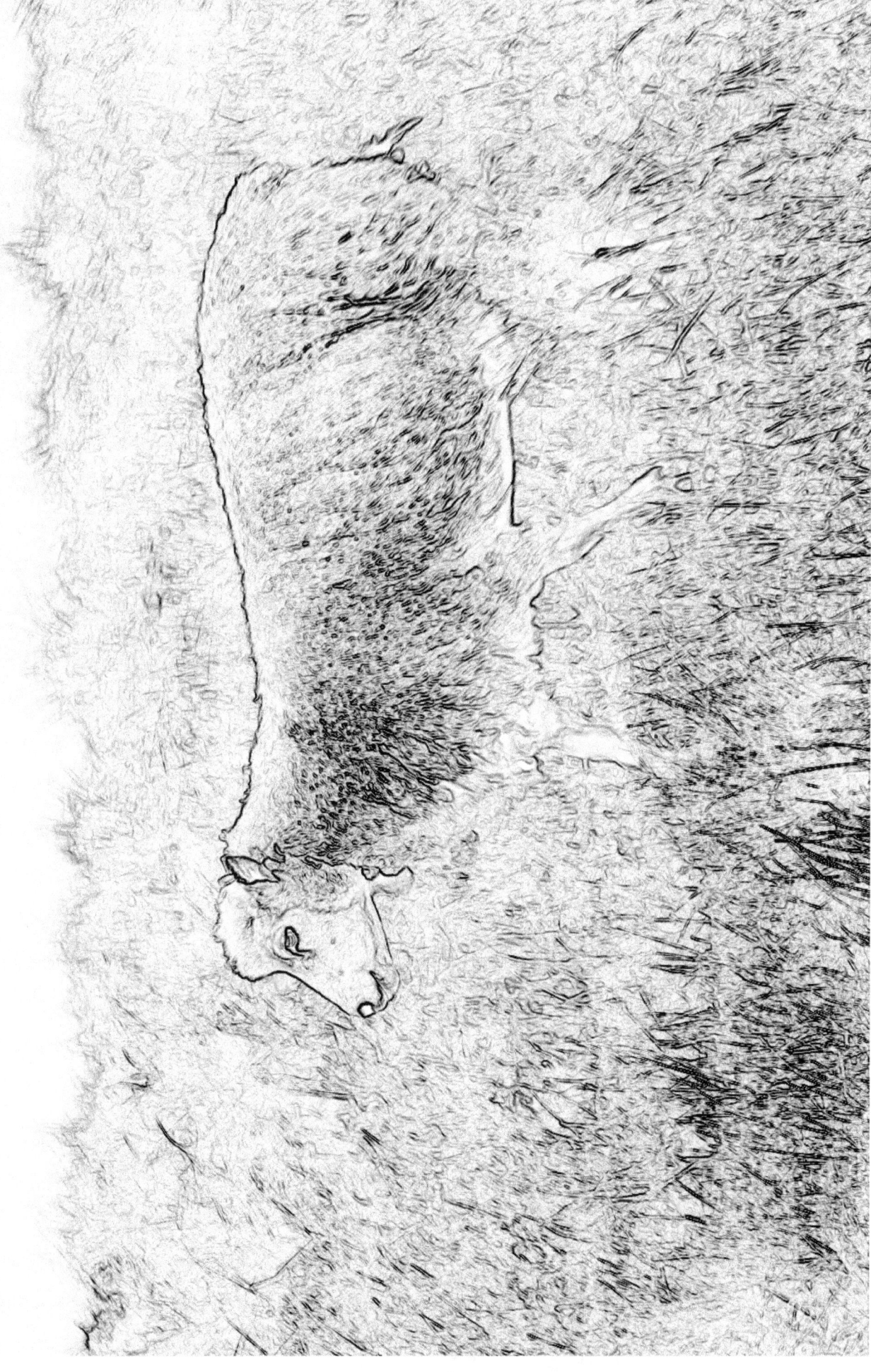

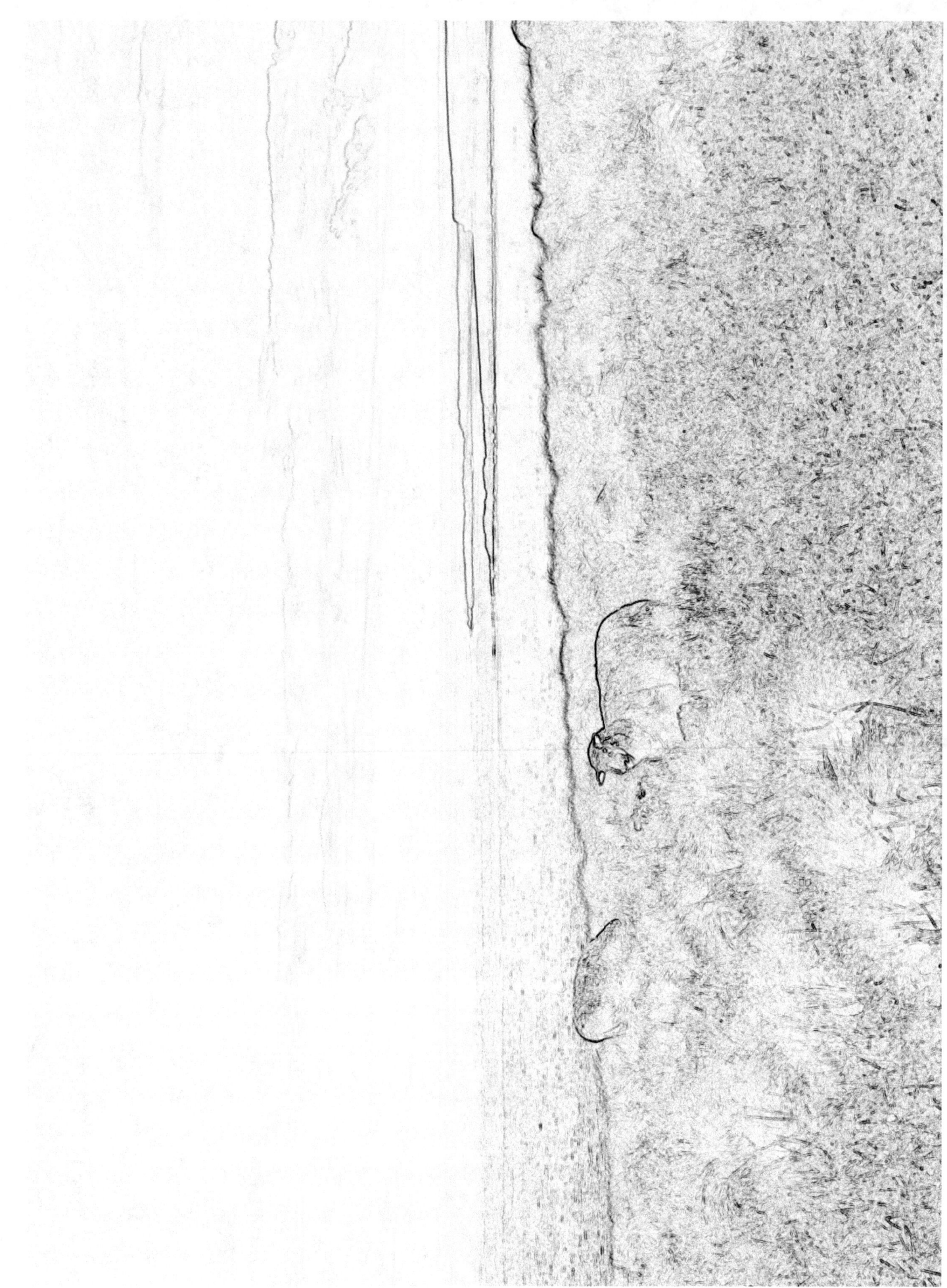

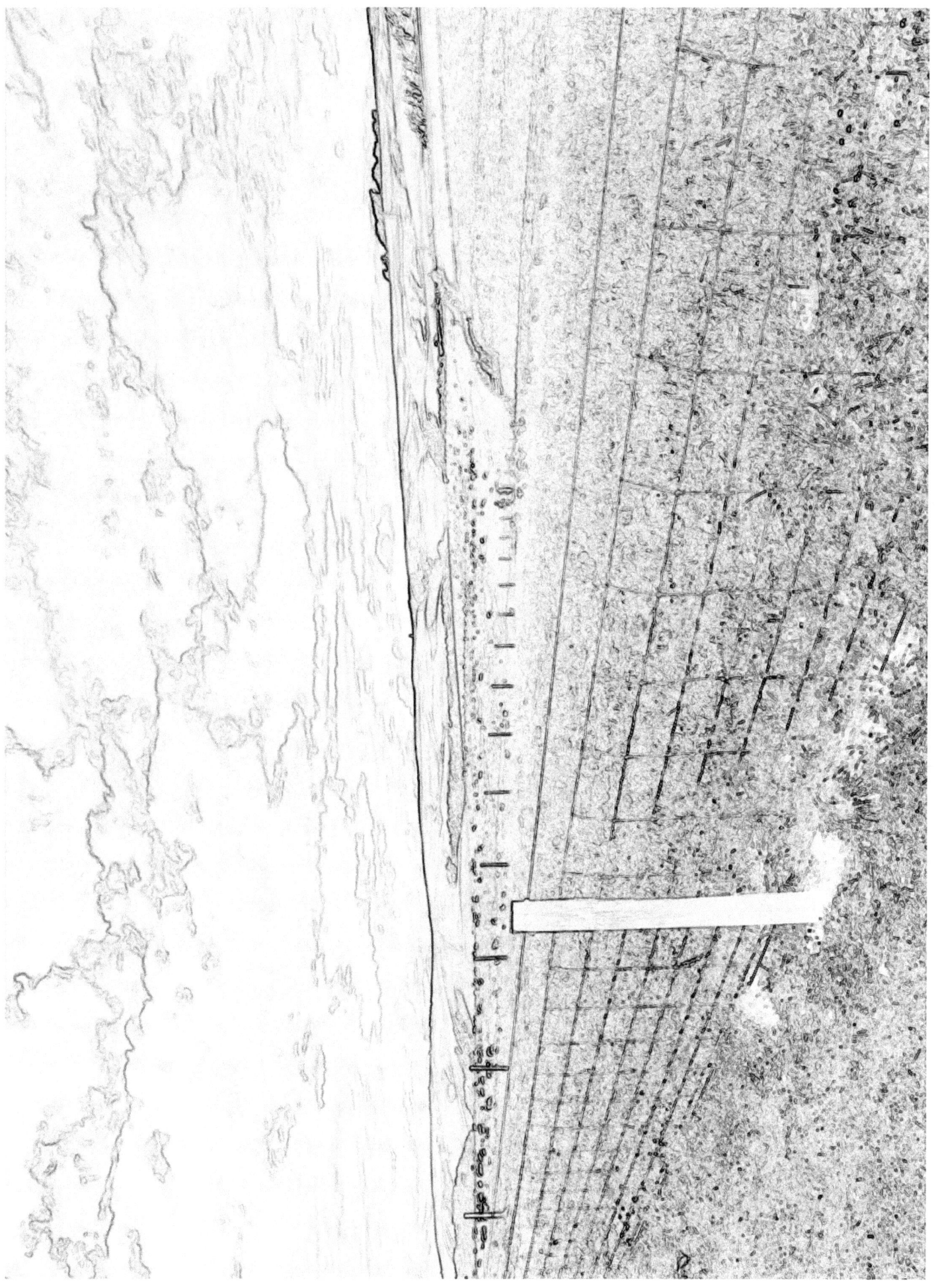

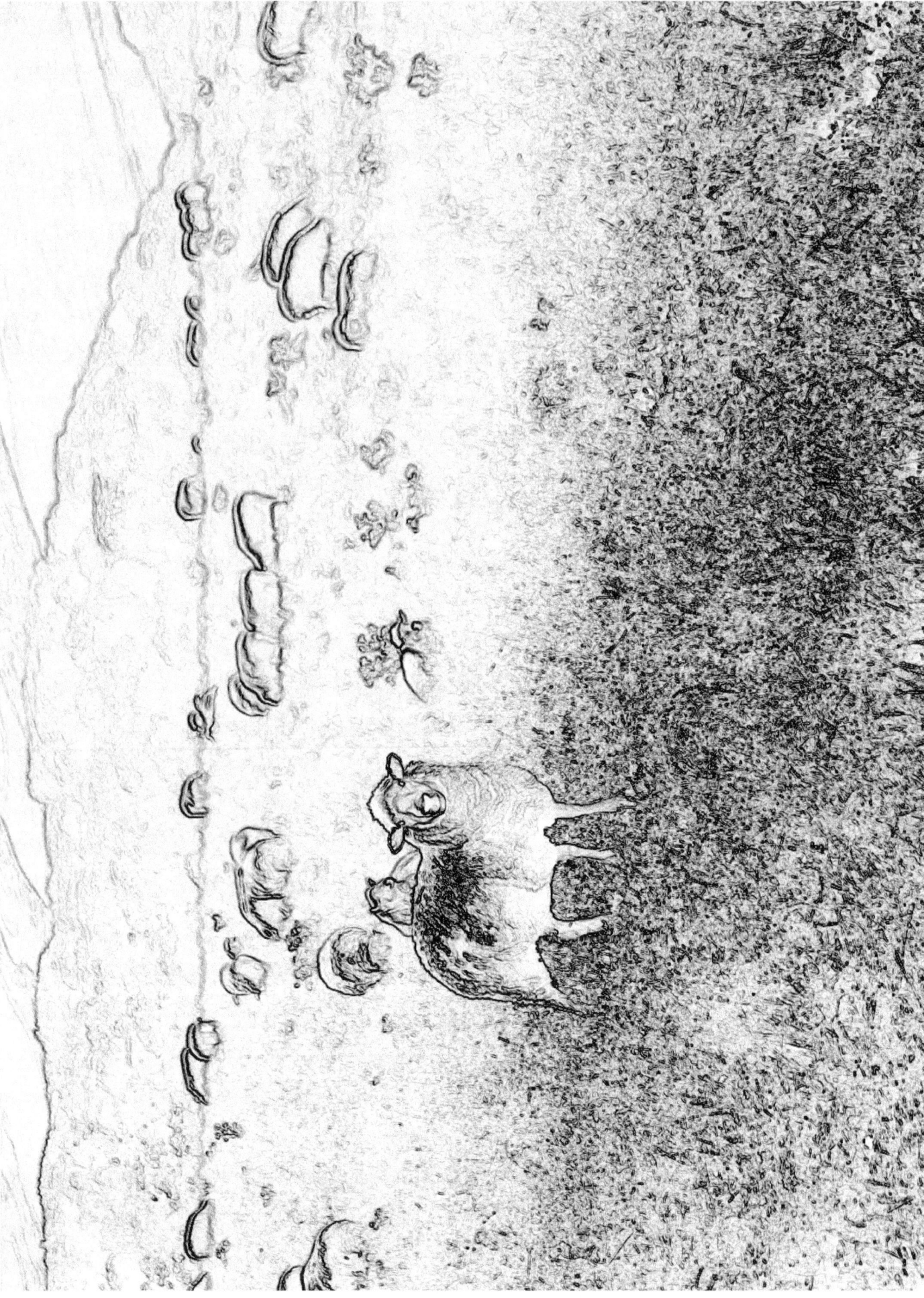

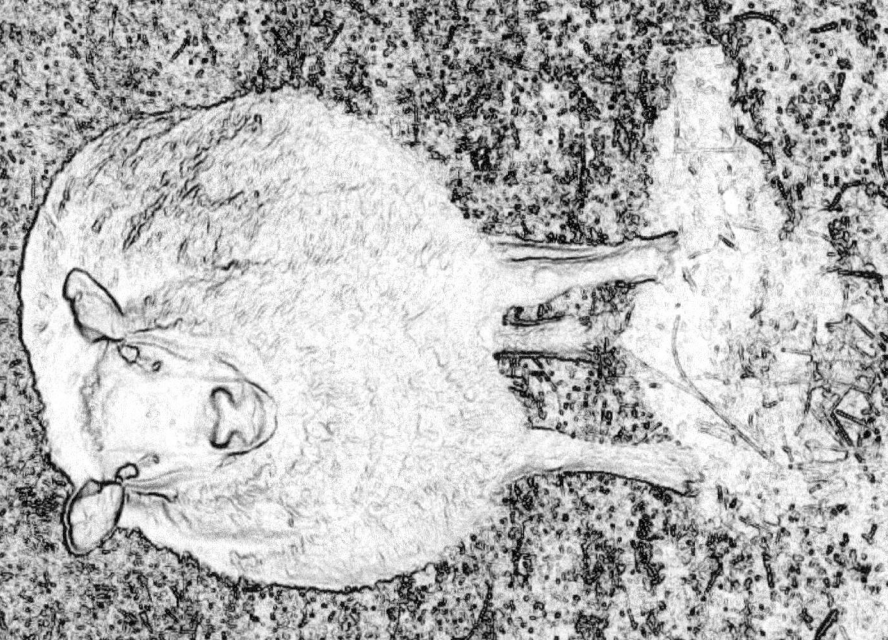

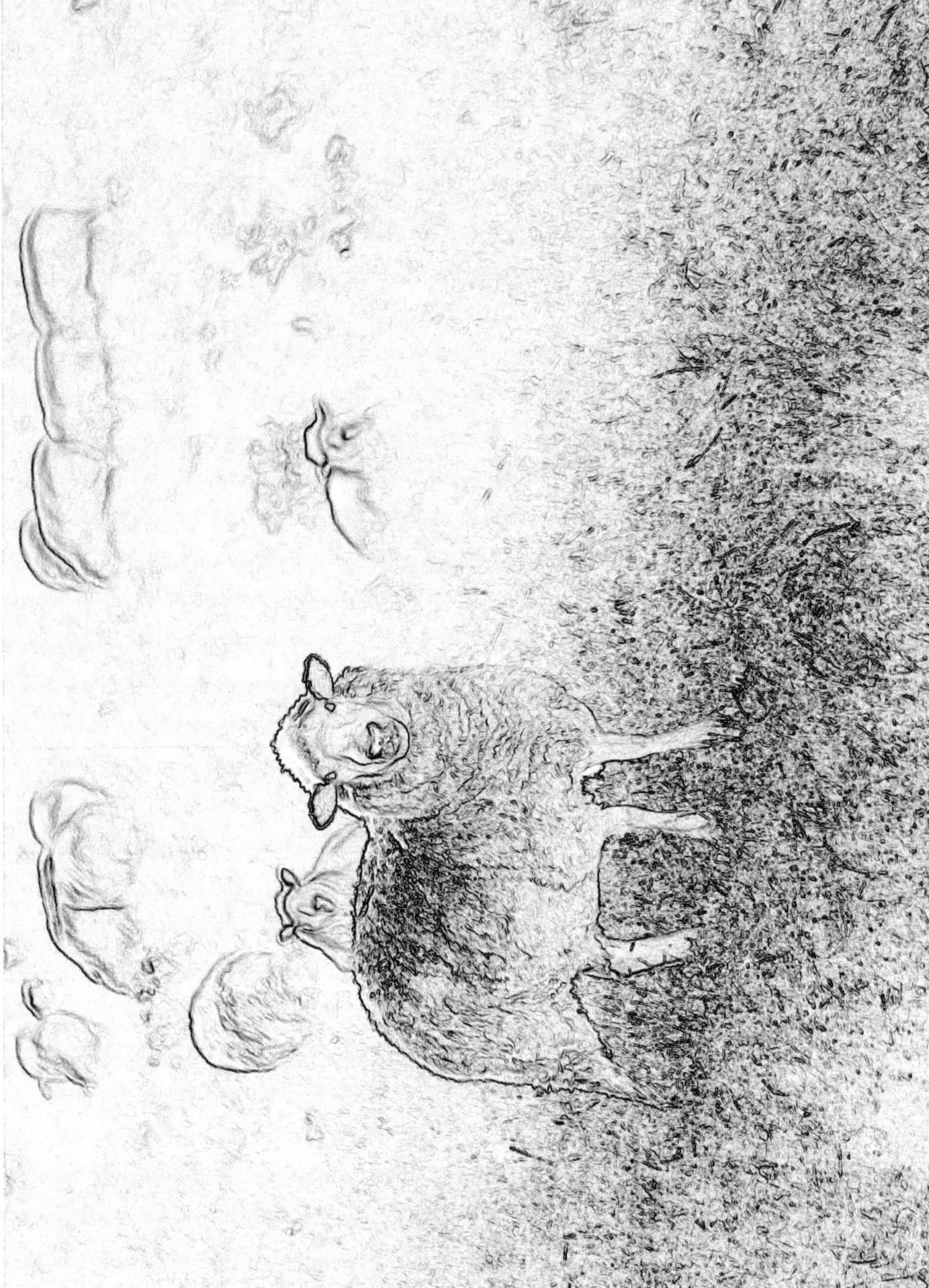

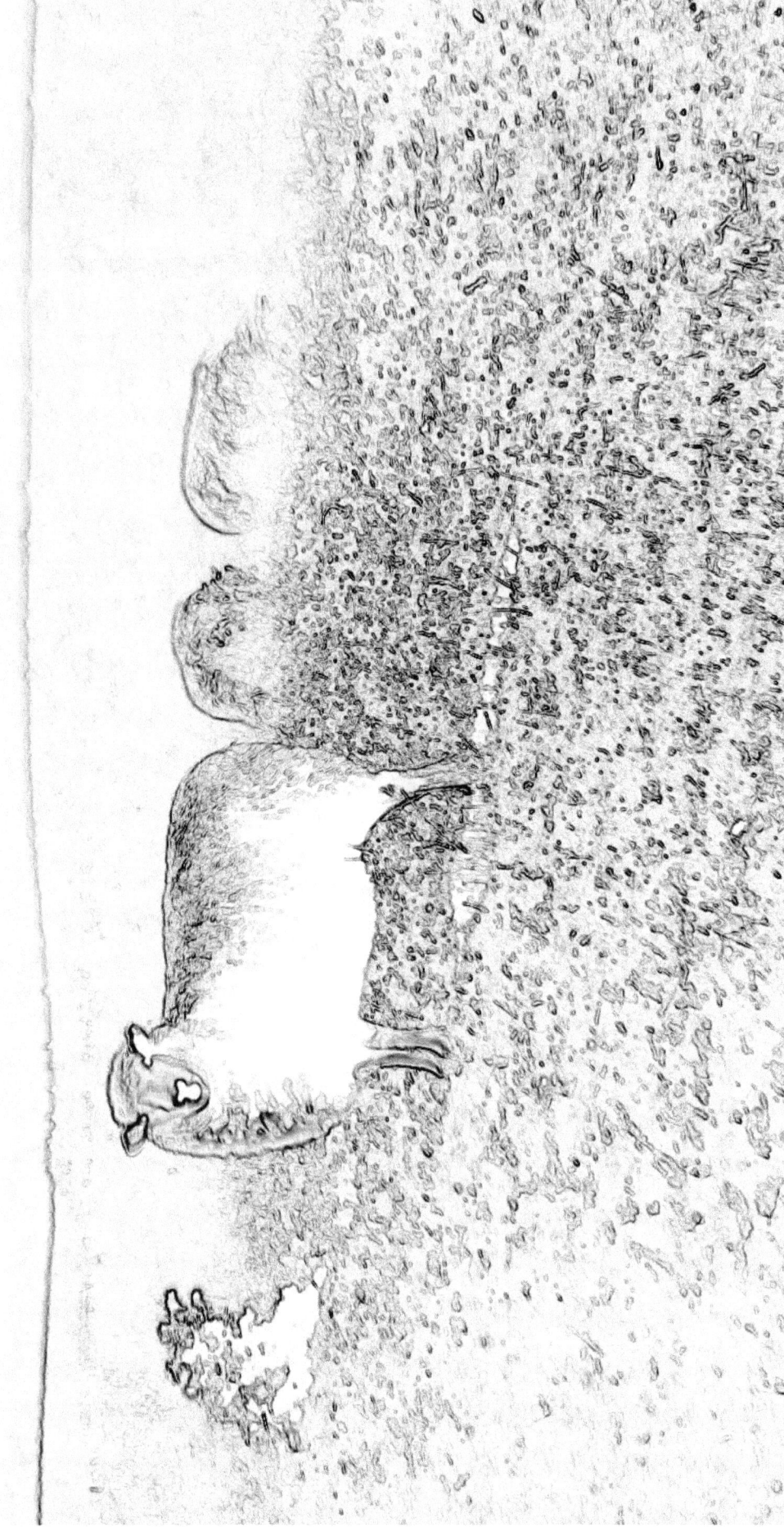

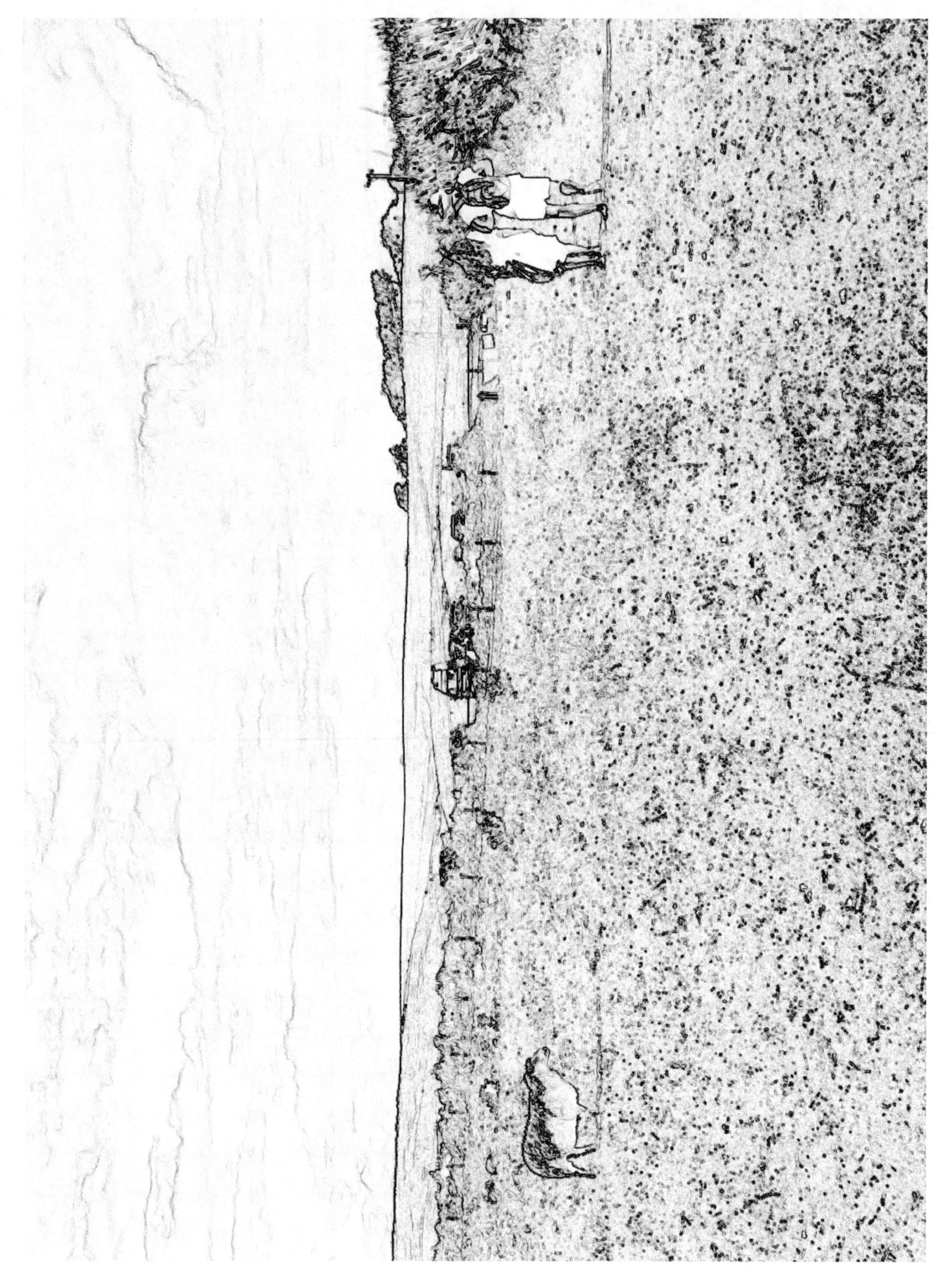

www.ingramcontent.com/pod-product-compliance
Lightning Source LLC
Chambersburg PA
CBHW080820220526

45466CB00011BB/3630